Beaded Friendship Bracelets

Mud Puddle Books

NEW YORK

Copyright © 2007 by

Mud Puddle Books, Inc.

54 W. 21st Street Suite 601

New York, NY 10010

info@mudpuddlebooks.com

ISBN: 978-1-59412-203-3

Printed in China

Table of Contents

Introduction

What exactly is a friend? Webster's dictionary defines "friend" as someone who is not an enemy. To us, friends can be classmates, roommates, companions, confidantes, soul mates, allies, collaborators, teammates, peers, or supporters. A friend is a person that helps you, encourages you, questions you when she is in doubt, has fun with you, works with you, stands by you when you need her, and finally, needs you as much as you need her. A friend can be a casual friend, a good friend, a close friend, or your very best friend.

A friend is a person you want to do something nice for, whether it's a special occasion like their birthday, or just because it's Tuesday and you feel like it. A friend is a person that you want to thank in a "you're special to me" sort of hand-made way.

That is why making friendship bracelets—for a friend or with a friend—is so much more meaningful than something store-bought. It's a special gift that you made with her in mind, something just for her. Remember, if it is made by hand, it comes from the heart.

Friendship bracelets are easy, fun, and inexpensive. You can make one or one hundred! Making unique bracelets for any occasion is simple—make them casual or dressy; beaded or plain; or from thread, ribbons, or strips of fabric. Your imagination is all you need to be a designer extraordinaire of friendship bracelets.

Supplies

Thread or Floss:

Traditional six-strand embroidery thread, usually called embroidery floss, is most often used to make friendship bracelets.

Specialty Fibers:

Pearl Cotton, knitting yarns, thin ribbons, soft silk-like fabrics, and specialty threads of any type can be used to make friendship bracelets.

Designer Secret: The colors and textures of specialty fibers add a "designer touch" to even a simple project. Use them by themselves, or mix-and-match to make a variety of bracelets.

Clipboard:

This book will refer to using a Knotting Board (see page 7), but you may prefer to use a clipboard rather than cardboard and pins to hold your bracelet while you are making it. This will secure the bracelet at the top, but you will be unable to pin the knots in place as you work.

Knotting Board:

We recommend creating a Knotting Board by using a thick piece of cardboard—such as the side of a box—to use as a work surface for creating your friendship bracelets. The board should be firm, yet allow you to easily insert and remove pins. Use large hatpins to secure your knots in place.

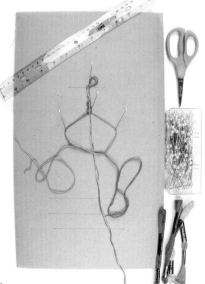

Tips

By marking the end length of your bracelet on the Knotting Board or clipboard, you will know at a glance just how long the bracelet needs to be.

Beads:

Beads of any type and size can be used to embellish your friendship bracelets. You will want to make certain that the thread or fiber you are using will fit through the hole of the bead. If you have difficulty getting the thread through the bead hole, you can use a Beading Wire Loop (see page 8) to help you. If the bead hole is just too small, try adding a length of thin, 24-guage wire to your threads. The beads will easily slip onto the wire.

Beading Wire Loop:

This loop is optional, but can make it easier to add beads to your bracelet. Simply take a thin piece of 24-gauge wire, bend, and wrap as shown in diagram.

Diagram

Embellishments:

Just about anything can be used to adorn friendship bracelets. Charms for jewelry-making, small craft items such as miniature Christmas garlands, or a multitude of scrapbooking embellishments can be added. Walk up and down the aisles of your favorite fabric or craft store and see all the wonderful things that can be used.

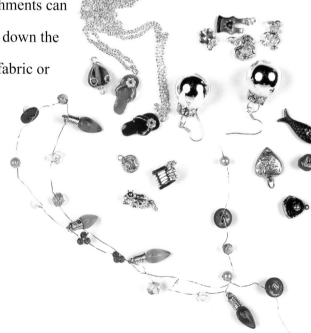

Jewelry Closures:

Jewelry closures are optional; however, they make removing your friendship bracelet a snap! See Ending Your Bracelet on page 14.

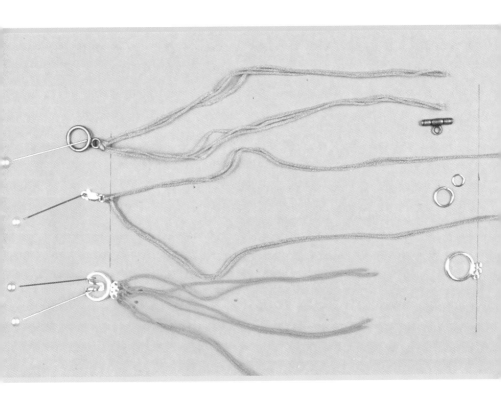

Miscellaneous Tools and Materials:

24-Gauge Beading Wire

Fabric Glue

Ruler

Scissors

Basic Knots

There are 3 basic knots used to make the friendship bracelets in this book. They are easy to master and easy to remember, but you may want to practice a little before beginning to make your first friendship bracelet. A little practice now will save a considerable amount of frustration, time, and materials.

Square Knot

This knot requires 3 to 4 threads to complete.

Step 1

Place the #4 thread on the far right over and to the left of the #2 and #3 center threads. Drop thread #4.

Step 2

Place thread #1 on top of thread #4.

Step 3

Bring thread #1 under the two center threads and through the loop on the right.

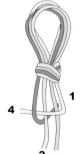

Step 4

Gently pull on threads #1 and #4 to tighten. The first half of the Square Knot is now complete. The second half of the Square Knot is the same only in reverse.

Step 5

Thread #4 is now on the left. Place thread #4 over and to the right of the #2 and #3 center threads. Drop thread #4.

Step 6

Place thread #1 on top of thread #4.

Step 7

Bring thread #1 under the two center threads and through the loop on the left.

Step 8

Gently pull on threads #1 and #4 to tighten. Your Square Knot is now complete.

Overhand Knot

This knot can be created with as few as 2 threads, but you can use as many threads as you like.

Right Overhand Knot

Step 1

Tightly hold the left-hand thread and knot the remaining thread around it.

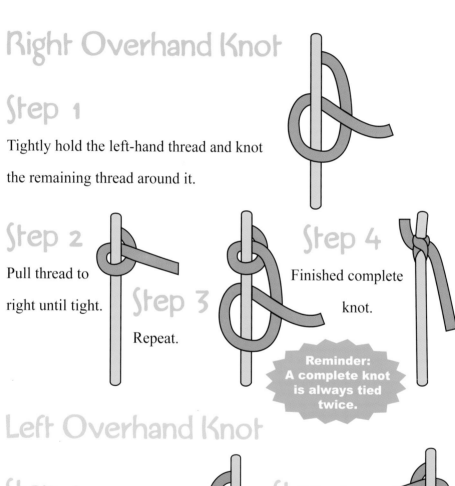

Step 2

Pull thread to right until tight.

Step 3

Repeat.

Step 4

Finished complete knot.

Reminder: A complete knot is always tied twice.

Left Overhand Knot

Step 1

Tightly hold the right-hand thread and knot the remaining thread around it.

Step 2

Pull thread to left until tight.

Step 3

Repeat.

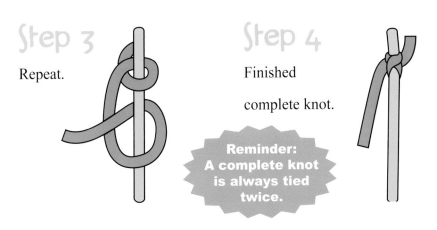

Step 4

Finished

complete knot.

**Reminder:
A complete knot
is always tied
twice.**

Note: In this book the Overhand Knot is sometimes completed as a Right Overhand Knot and sometimes as a Left Overhand Knot, but either way it is the same knot. The Overhand Knot can be made with as many threads as you want.

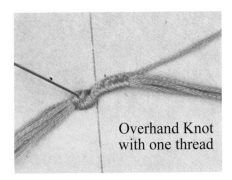

Overhand Knot
with one thread

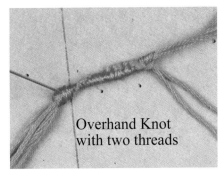

Overhand Knot
with two threads

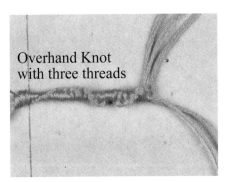

Overhand Knot
with three threads

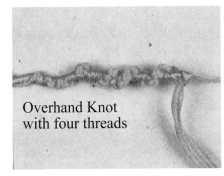

Overhand Knot
with four threads

Ending Your Bracelet

Each of the projects in this book tells you how to end the bracelet as it is pictured in the example. However, the following endings can be used with any of the bracelets you learn to make, so feel free to make any substitutions.

Possibility 1: Looped End Bracelet

Folding the threads in half when starting the bracelet will create a loop at one end that can be used for tying bracelet ends together.

TO WEAR: Wrap the finished bracelet around your wrist. Divide the threads at the loose end, and slip one half of the threads through the loop. Tie to the other half of the threads, securing in a double knot so that bracelet does not come untied.

Tips

Fastening your bracelets with Possibility 1 or Possibility 2 is best for those that will be worn until you tire of them. Tying and untying the threads will eventually fray them, making it difficult to tie a secure knot.

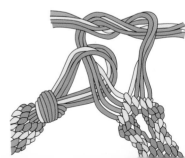

Possibility 2: Loose Ends Bracelet

This bracelet is made by using single strands of thread that are not folded in half and looped.

TO WEAR: Wrap the finished bracelet around your wrist. Tie ends together in a double knot, cutting longer ends to desired length.

Possibility 3: Jewelry Closure Bracelet

These bracelets have jewelry closures at both ends just like traditional jewelry, making it possible to remove the bracelet as often as desired.

The closures are easiest to attach when the bracelet is made from 3 or 4 strands of embroidery floss. After tying the closures to the bracelet ends, you may need to place a small amount of fabric glue over the knots to keep them secure.

TO WEAR: Attach this bracelet to your wrist just as you would attach any piece of traditional jewelry.

Projects

The projects found in this book employ the fun and easy techniques you have already learned. Just follow the step-by-step instructions to create fabulous designs for your and your friends.

Note: If you are a user of the metric system, simply multiply any of the measurements used in this book by 2.54 to determine the centimeters.

Basic Wrapped Bracelet

This easy bracelet requires a flexible core thread to wrap the threads of the bracelet around. Mix up the size of your bracelets by using a thin or thick core—it all just depends on the bracelet you want to create!

Materials:

Core thread, thin

Embroidery floss, 1 color

Step 1

Cut core thread to desired length of finished
bracelet. Cut 2 strands of embroidery floss to
4 times the length of the core thread, tie both
strands of floss to the core. Be sure to leave
a long enough tail to tie your bracelet onto
your wrist.

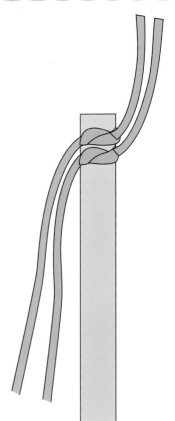

Step 2

Pin the core thread to the Knotting Board. Tightly wrap both strands
of floss around the core thread to the end and tie in a knot.

Step 3

Wrap finished bracelet around wrist and tie floss ends together in a
double knot. If ends are too long, trim to desired length.

Wrapped Bracelet with Alternating Colors

Want to add a little variety to your bracelets? This simple bracelet alternates colors to let you and your friends show off your favorite colors, school pride, or any other color combination!

Materials:

Core thread, thin

Embroidery floss, 2 colors

Step 1

Cut core thread to desired length of finished bracelet. Cut each color of embroidery floss to 8 times the length of the core thread. Fold floss in half, cut in two, and tie all four lengths of floss to the core. Be sure to leave a long enough tail to tie your bracelet onto your wrist.

Step 2

Pin the core thread to the Knotting Board. Tightly wrap the two strands of the first color of floss around the core and the second color of floss until you have the desired amount of color.

Step 3

Pick up the strands of the second color floss and tightly wrap around both the core thread and the first color of floss until you have the desired amount of color.

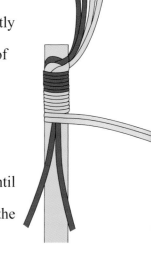

Step 4

Repeat Steps 2 and 3, alternating colors as desired until you reach the end of the core thread. Knot tightly at the end of the core thread.

Step 5

Wrap finished bracelet around wrist and tie floss ends together in a double knot. If ends are too long, trim to desired length.

Wrapped Bracelet with Cord Wrap

Materials:

Colored thin cord, 1 color

Core thread, thin

Embroidery floss, 1 color

Step 1

Cut core thread to desired length of finished bracelet. Cut embroidery floss to 8 times the length of the core thread and colored cord to 3 times the length of the core thread. Fold floss in half, cut in two, and tie to the core thread, leaving a long enough tail to tie your bracelet to your wrist.

Step 2

Tie colored cord to the core thread directly beneath the floss.

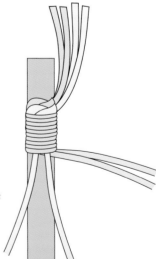

Step 3

Pin the core thread to the Knotting Board. Wrap the 2 embroidery floss strands around the core thread and colored cord for about ½".

Step 4

Pull the colored cord up and move it out the way. Continue wrapping core thread with embroidery floss to the end. Knot tightly at the end of the core thread.

colored cord

floss

Step 5

Twist colored cord strands together and wrap the colored cord around the floss-wrapped core. When the cord reaches the end of the solid color floss, tie cord in a tight knot.

Step 6

Wrap finished bracelet around wrist and tie floss ends together in a double knot. If ends are too long, trim to desired length.

Basic Wrapped Bracelet with Cord Beads

Materials:

Core thread, thin

Embroidery floss, 1 color

(Example uses variegated pink floss)

Metallic cords

This bracelet is made by following the steps for the Basic Wrapped Bracelet on page 16, using floss over the core thread. When core thread is completely wrapped, wrap metallic cord over the floss at various intervals to resemble a bead. Once the desired amount of cord has been wrapped, tie a knot, clip the ends of the cord, and move down the core thread to where the next "bead" should be wrapped.

Basic Wrapped Bracelet Using Novelty Fibers

Materials:

Core thread, thin

Novelty fiber(s)

These bracelets are made by following the steps for the Basic Wrapped Bracelet on page 16. Simply wrap the core thread with the novelty fiber(s) of your choice.

Designer Style: To make the pink and aqua bracelet, or to use any other desired color combination, follow the instruction for Wrapped Bracelet with Alternating Colors on page 18.

Basic Wrapped Bracelet with Beads

Materials:

Beads, 1 or more colors

Core thread, thin

Embroidery floss, 1 color

Fabric glue (Optional)

These bracelets are made by following the
steps for the Basic Wrapped Bracelet on
page 16. After wrapping core thread
with desired color of floss, slip beads
onto the bracelet. If beads need to
be further secured into place,
tie a piece of floss or a thin
ribbon just below the bead
or beaded section,

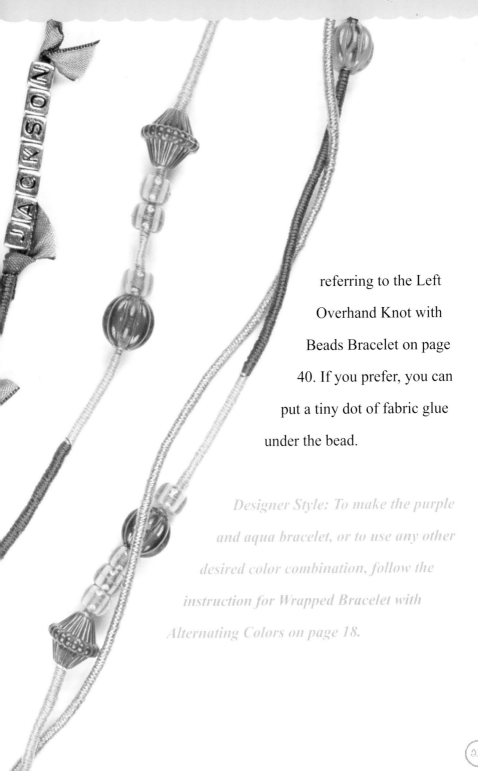

referring to the Left Overhand Knot with Beads Bracelet on page 40. If you prefer, you can put a tiny dot of fabric glue under the bead.

Designer Style: To make the purple and aqua bracelet, or to use any other desired color combination, follow the instruction for Wrapped Bracelet with Alternating Colors on page 18.

Basic Wrapped Bracelet with Silk Ribbon

Materials:

Core thread, thick

Silk ribbon

This bracelet is made by following the steps for the Basic Wrapped Bracelet on page 16. Simply wrap the core thread with silk ribbon. Tie a second length of silk ribbon to wrapped bracelet and rewrap the bracelet using loose, uneven wraps.

Basic Wrapped Bracelet with Separate Bead Strand

Materials:

24-gauge wire

Assorted beads

Core thread, thin

Metallic thread

This bracelet is made by following the steps for the Basic Wrapped Bracelet on page 16. Cut a length of wire 2" longer than the completed wrap and string with a variety of beads. Wrap the wire around the wrapped core thread at both ends until secure, then tie a double knot.

Twist and Shout!

Materials:

Embroidery floss, 10 lengths—28" each

(Example uses variegated green floss)

Step 1

Tie all 10 floss strands in a
knot, leaving a long enough
tail to tie the bracelet to your
wrist. Fasten the knot to the
Knotting Board.

Step 2

Hold the loose ends
of the floss together
and twist them several
times until they are
very tight.

Step 3

Pull the twisted strands straight and place your finger in the center of the twisted length. Fold the twisted strands in half and remove your finger.

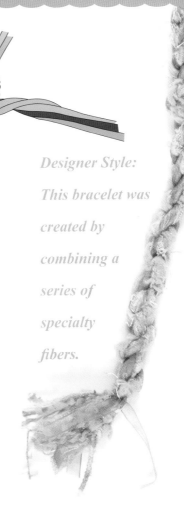

Designer Style: This bracelet was created by combining a series of specialty fibers.

Step 4

Remove the rope from your Knotting Board and knot the free ends together to create a double-knot effect. Trim uneven threads.

Step 5

Wrap finished bracelet around wrist. Divide the strands at the unlooped end of the bracelet, and slip half of the strands through the loop. Tie strand ends in a double knot so that your bracelet will not come untied.

Braided Thread Bracelet

Materials:

Embroidery floss, 3 colors

Silk-like fabric, coordinating color

Step 1

Measure 3 colors of floss to 6 times the desired length of finished bracelet. Fold in half and knot 1" from fold. Pin to the Knotting Board and braid to desired length of bracelet.

1 2 3

1 3 2

3 1

2

2

3 1

Step 2

Cut fabric into a 1"-wide strip the same length as the bracelet. Place braided floss on top of fabric strip. Just below the knot at the bracelet loop, tie a piece of floss around both the braided bracelet and the fabric strip, then knot. Leave a tail on the wrap just long enough to tie a second knot.

Step 3

Wrap finished bracelet around wrist. Push the plain end of the bracelet through the loop, wrap with floss tail, and tie a slipknot for easy removal.

Star Weave Bracelet

Materials:

Beads

Embroidery floss, 2 colors

(Example uses red and orange)

Step 1

Measure and cut two 34" lengths of both floss colors. Fold all lengths in half and knot 1" from fold. Pin knot to Knotting Board and separate floss by color so that all of one color are on the right side and all of the second color are on the left side.

1   2   3   4

Step 2

Beginning with the far right pair of #4 floss strands, take them under the pair of #3 threads next to them, as well as under the #2 pair. Bring the threads back over the #2 pair, leaving these strands in the middle.

Step 3

Picking up the #1 pair of threads on the far left that have not yet been used, take them under the #2 threads next to them, as well as under the #4 pair. Bring these threads back over the #4 threads, leaving these strands in the middle.

1   2 4

Step 4

Pull the pairs of threads tightly to the top. Repeat Steps 2 and 3 for approximately half the length of your bracelet.

2   1   4

Step 5

Add a bead to the desired pair of threads, and continue weaving until you reach the end.

Step 6

Tie all threads into a knot at the end. String on 2 more beads, then tie a second knot to secure beads. Cut threads so they are even.

2

1 4

Step 7

Wrap finished bracelet around wrist. Divide the threads at the unlooped end of the bracelet, and slip half of the threads through the loop. Tie thread ends in a doubt knot so that your bracelet will not come untied.

Woven Bracelet with Beads

Materials:

24-gauge wire, 34"

Embroidery floss, 2 colors

(Example uses blue and green)

Small beads

String beads onto wire. Following the steps for the Star Weave Bracelet on page 31, weave the beaded wire into your bracelet by including it with one of the sections of floss strands. It doesn't matter which pair of threads you add the wire to, just keep the wire with the same pair of threads as you weave.

1-2-3 Bracelet

Materials:

Pearl Cotton thread, 3 colors

Step 1

Cut a length of the first color thread to 56". Cut one length
of each of the remaining colors to 18". Tie all three
lengths of thread together and pin knot to the Knotting
Board, then separate threads as shown in diagram.

Step 2

Weave the #3 thread over the #2 thread and under
the #1 thread, then over the #1 and under the #2
thread. Be careful to hold the threads straight
and tight while you weave.

Step 3

Hold the #1 and #2 threads with one hand and
pull the #3 thread so that the weaving slides up
the bracelet toward the top knot. Continue
weaving for approximately 1".

Step 4

Repeat Steps 2 and 3, but instead of pulling the #3 thread tight, leave it loose. Continue weaving for approximately another 1" or so.

Step 5

Continue weaving sections that alternate tight weaves and loose weaves until the bracelet is complete.

Step 6

Tie a knot at the end of the bracelet.

Step 7

Wrap finished bracelet around wrist and tie thread ends together in a double knot. If ends are too long, trim to desired length.

Designer Style: One bracelet was woven from Pearl Cotton threads and the other from very tiny grosgrain ribbon. While this bracelet can be made from embroidery floss, the finished bracelet will be much more delicate.

Left Overhand Knotted Bracelet

Materials:

Embroidery floss, 4 colors

Step 1

Measure floss to 3 times the desired length of finished bracelet, cut, and tie a knot approximately 2" from the end. Pin knot to the Knotting Board.

Step 2

Separating the thread on the far left from the others, hold the remaining 3 threads together. Knot the single thread on the far left around them using the left Overhand Knot. Repeat until you have six complete Overhand Knots.

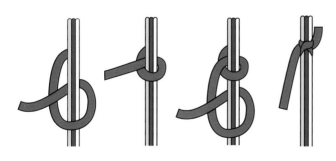

Reminder: A complete knot is always tied twice.

Step 3

Place the knotting thread into the center group of threads. Take the second color thread, which is now on the far left, and continue knotting.

Step 4

Repeat Steps 2 and 3, alternating colors as desired.

Step 5

Tie a knot at the end of the bracelet.

Step 6

Wrap finished bracelet around wrist and simply tie the two knotted ends together.

Designer Style: For a variation, you can add beads onto the knotting thread at random intervals.

Left Overhand Knot With Braids

Materials:

Embroidery thread, 3 colors

Step 1

Measure each color to 3 times the desired length of finished bracelet, cut, and tie a knot approximately 2" from the end. Pin knot to the Knotting Board.

Step 2

Separating the thread on the far left from the others, hold the remaining 5 threads together. Knot the single thread on the far left around them to make 10 complete Left Overhand Knots.

Reminder: A complete knot is always tied twice.

Step 3

Divide the threads into three groups according to color.

Step 4

Braid the 3 colors of thread together

until the braid is the desired length.

Step 5

Gather all of the strings together,

pulling out one thread that is

a different color from the first

thread that was used for knotting.

Step 6

Repeat steps 2 to 5 until the bracelet is the desired length. Knot the end.

Step 7

Wrap bracelet around your wrist and tie the two knotted ends together.

Left Overhand Knot with Beads

Materials:

Assorted beads

Embroidery floss or Pearl Cotton thread

These bracelets are made by following the steps for the Left Overhand Knotted Bracelet on page 36.

1 To make bracelet #1, measure and cut 2 strands of floss to 6 times the desired length of finished bracelet. Fold in half, knot 1" from loop, and pin to the Knotting Board. Knot 3 of the strands over 1 strand. Slip beads onto bracelet in between knots, spelling your friend's name, or anything else you wish.

2 To make bracelet #2, measure and cut 2 strands of cording to 10 times the desired length of finished bracelet. Fold in half, knot 1" from loop, and pin to the Knotting Board. Knot one cord over the other, adding beads as desired.

3 To make bracelet #3, measure and cut 5 strands of 4 colors of embroidery floss 4 times the desired length of finished bracelet (cut 2 lengths of 1 color of floss). Tie a knot approximately 2" from the end. Alternate colors as desired until the final quarter of the bracelet. To finish, simply knot the four different colors over the 1 remaining strand of the duplicate color and knot end. Add beads throughout as desired.

Left Overhand Knot with Beads on Wire

Materials:

24-gauge wire, 34"

Assorted beads

Embroidery floss, 1 color

String wire with beads. Measure and cut 3 strands of the same color floss to 6 times the desired length of finished bracelet and knot approximately 2" from end. Follow the directions for the Left Overhand Knotted Bracelet on page 36, adding the beaded wire to one of the threads. It does not matter which thread you add the wire to, just keep the wire with the same thread as you weave.

Basic Diagonal Stripe Bracelet

Materials:

Embroidery floss, 4 colors

Step 1

Measure and cut 1 strand of each color floss to 6 times the desired length of finished bracelet. Tie a knot 2" from the top and pin to the Knotting Board.

Step 2

Separate the strands.

Step 3

1 2 3 4

Beginning with the #1 thread on the far left , tie a complete Overhand Knot over thread #2.

Reminder: A complete knot is always tied twice.

Step 4

Continuing with strand #1, make a complete Overhand Knot around each of the remaining threads.

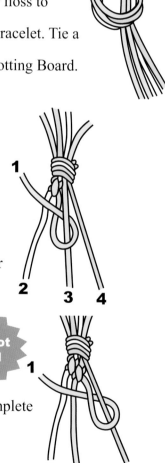

42

Tips

Hold each thread that is being tied straight and tight,
pulling each knot you make to the same degree of snugness.
This will give your finished bracelet a consistent texture.

Step 5

Your #2 thread should now be at the far left. Begin the
process again, tying complete Overhand Knots over each
of the #3, #4, and #1 strands to the right.

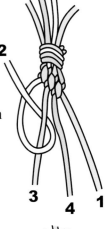

Step 6

Continue knotting your threads in this manner until
bracelet is of desired length.

Step 7

Tie a knot at the end of your bracelet. Trim the remaining
thread to approximately 2".

Step 8

Wrap finished bracelet around wrist and tie the two knotted
ends together.

Variation on Diagonal Stripe

Materials:

Embroidery floss, 2 colors

Measure and cut 1 strand of each color floss to 6 times the desired length of finished bracelet. Fold in half, tie a knot 1" from the fold, and pin to the Knotting Board. Follow the directions for the Basic Diagonal Stripe Bracelet on page 42, alternating between 2 colors instead of 4.

Variation on Diagonal Stripe 2

Materials:

Embroidery floss, 2 colors
Pearl Cotton thread, 1 color

Measure and cut 1 strand of each color of floss and Pearl Cotton to 6 times the desired length of finished bracelet. Fold in half, tie a knot 1" from the fold, and pin to the Knotting Board. Follow the directions for the Basic Diagonal Stripe Bracelet on page 42, alternating between 3 colors.

Variation on Diagonal Stripe 3

Materials:

Pearl Cotton thread, 2 colors

Measure and cut 3 strands of each color thread to 3 times the desired length of finished bracelet. Tie a knot 2" from the top and pin to the Knotting Board. Follow directions for the Basic Diagonal Stripe Bracelet on page 42, tying the first 10 rows of Overhand Knots with 2 strands of thread, the next 10 rows with 1 strand of thread, and the next 10 rows with 2 strands of thread. Alternate this pattern until bracelet is of desired length.

Variation on Diagonal Stripe 4

Materials:

Embroidery floss, 3 colors   (Example uses: white, grey, blue)

Measure and cut 1 strand of each color floss to 6 times the desired length of finished bracelet. Fold in half, tie a knot 1" from the fold, and pin to the Knotting Board. Separate thread so that the color order is as follows: 1 strand white, 2 strands grey, 1 strand white, 2 strands blue. Follow the directions for the Basic Diagonal Stripe Bracelet on page 42, alternating between 3 colors.

Variation on Diagonal Stripe 5

Materials:

Embroidery floss, 1 color   (Example uses: pink floss,
Metallic thread, 1 color   metallic silver thread)

Measure and cut 2 strands of each color thread to 6 times the desired length of finished bracelet. Fold in half, tie a knot 1" from the fold, and pin to the Knotting Board. Follow directions for the Basic Diagonal Stripe Bracelet on page 42, alternating between 2 colors.

Diagonal Stripe with Beads

Materials:

24-gauge wire

Embroidery floss, 4 colors

Glass beads

Measure and cut 1 strand of each color floss to 3 times the desired length of finished bracelet. Measure and cut 1 length of wire 2 times the desired length of finished bracelet. Tie a knot 2" from top and pin to the Knotting Board. Follow the directions for the Basic Diagonal Stripe Bracelet on page 42, carrying the wire with one of the threads being knotted around. Add beads to the wire as desired, carrying the wire with one of the threads being knotted around when no beads are desired.

Note: Do NOT carry the wire with one of the threads making the knots, as this will be too difficult and the wire will show in the finished bracelet.

Basic Chevron Bracelet

Materials:

Pearl Cotton thread, 4 colors

Note: Although the Chevron Bracelet can be made with other types of threads, a heavier Pearl Cotton thread, will make it easier to see the stripes.

Step 1

Measure 1 thread of each color to 6 times the desired length of finished bracelet. Fold in half and tie a knot 1" from loop. Pin to the Knotting Board.

Step 2

Separate threads as shown in diagram.

Reminder: A complete knot is always tied twice.

Step 3

1 2 3 4 4 3 2 1

Take the #1 thread that is on the far left and, working to the center, make a complete Overhand Knot onto threads #2, #3, and #4. Stop knotting and leave thread #1 in the center.

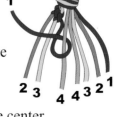

Step 4

Take the #1 thread that is on the far right and, working to the center, make a complete Overhand Knot onto threads #2, #3, and #4.

Step 5

Tie the two middle #1 threads together using a complete Overhand Knot.

Step 6

Beginning with the outermost threads and working toward the center, repeat Steps 3 to 5. Continue tying until bracelet is the desired length.

Step 7

Tie a knot at the end of the bracelet.

Step 8

Wrap finished bracelet around wrist, slip the loose ends through the loop, and tie a knot.

Chevron with Beads

Materials:

Beads, 6

Pearl Cotton thread, 4 colors

Measure and cut 2 strands of each color thread to 6 times the desired length of finished bracelet. Fold in half and knot approximately 1" from loop. Pin to the Knotting Board. Follow the directions for the Basic Chevron Bracelet on page 48, slipping beads over the 2 middle threads for the last 1½" of the bracelet.

Designer Style: This chevron design was created by wrapping over 2 threads at a time.

Divided Chevron Bracelet

Materials:

Pearl Cotton thread, 3 colors

Step 1

Measure and cut 1 strand of each color thread 6 times the desired length of finished bracelet. Fold in half and knot approximately 1" below loop. Pin to the Knotting Board.

Step 2

Separate threads as shown in diagram.

Reminder: A complete knot is always tied twice.

Step 3

Take the #1 thread that is on the far left and, working toward the center, make a complete Overhand Knot onto threads #2 and #3. Stop knotting and leave thread #1 in the center.

1 2   3 4   4 3   2 1

1

2 3 4   4 3 2 1   2 3 4 1   4 3 2 1

Step 4

Take the #1 thread that is on the far right and, working toward the center, make a complete Overhand Knot onto threads #2 , #3, and #4.

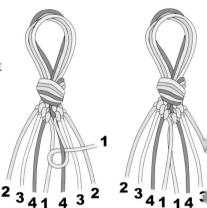

Step 5

Tie the two middle #1 threads together using a complete Overhand Knot.

Step 6

Beginning with the outermost threads and working toward the center, repeat Steps 3 to 5. Continue tying until bracelet is the desired length.

Step 7

Separate threads into 2 sections. Using left-hand thread #1, tie complete Overhand Knots onto left-hand

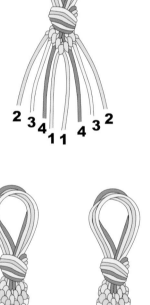

threads #2, #3 and #4. Repeat as many times as you like.

Step 8

Repeat Step 7 on the
right-hand side of the
bracelet.

Step 9

Separate threads, positioning them in their original
color order, and repeat Steps 3 to 6, then Steps 7 to 8 to
desired bracelet length.

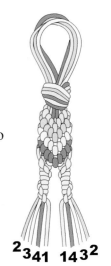

Step 10

Knot the end of the bracelet and trim tail to about 2".

Step 11

Wrap finished bracelet around wrist, slip the loose
ends through the loop, and tie a knot.

Variation on Divided Chevron

Materials:

Embroidery floss, 4 colors

Measure and cut 1 strand of each color embroidery floss to 6 times the desired length of finished bracelet. Fold in half and knot approximately 1" from loop. Pin to the Knotting Board. Following the directions for the Divided Chevron Bracelet on page 51, adding additional divisions as desired. Split the threads into two sections, with 1 thread of each color on either side. Starting with the left-hand group of threads, knot 1 thread over the remaining threads using a Left Overhand Knot for as long as desired. Repeat with the right-hand group of threads. Alternate between the Basic Chevron design and the Overhand Knot pattern until bracelet is desired length.

Variation on Divided Chevron 2

Materials:

Beads

Embroidery floss, 2 colors

Measure and cut 4 strands of each color floss to 3 times the desired length of finished bracelet. Knot threads 2" from end and pin to the Knotting Board. Follow directions for the Divided Chevron Bracelet on page 51, adding additional divisions as desired. Split the threads into 4 sections, string 2 beads onto each section, then combine threads into 2 sections. Create desired number of Overhand Knots on the left-hand side, then repeat for the right side. Split threads back into 4 sections, string 2 beads onto each section, then repeat Overhand Knot pattern. Split threads back into 4 sections, string 2 beads per section, then continue with the Basic Chevron design until desired bracelet length is reached. Tie a knot in the end.

Basic Square Knot Bracelet with Beads

Materials:

Assorted beads

Embroidery floss, 1 color

Sequin strand

Thin cording

Measure and cut 3 strands embroidery floss to 6 times the desired length of finished bracelet. Fold in half and knot approximately 1" from loop. Tie a knot. Pin to the Knotting Board. Following the directions for the Square Knot on page 10, make a series of square knots, then add 3 beads as shown. Make a second series of square knots, add 3 more beads, and finish with a final series of square knots. Measure and cut 1 strand of thin cording and 1 strand of sequins $1\frac{1}{2}$ times the desired length of finished bracelet. Holding the beaded bracelet, sequin strand, and thin cording together, knot a length of embroidery thread around one end and wrap together as shown. Repeat for other end.

Variation on Basic Square Knot with Beads

Materials:

Embroidery floss, 1 color

Wooden bead, large

Measure and cut 4 strands embroidery floss to 6 times
the desired length of finished bracelet. Fold in half
and knot approximately 1" from loop. Pin to the Knotting
Board. Following the directions for the Square Knot on
page 10, make a series of Square Knots, braid the floss
for approximately 1", then create another series of Square
Knots. Slip the bead onto the threads, then repeat knotting
and braiding to match first half of the bracelet.

Square Knot with Raised Picots

Materials:

Embroidery floss, 2 colors

Metal word plate

Step 1

Measure and cut 1 strand of each color thread to 4 times the desired length of finished bracelet. Fold in half, tie a knot approximately 1" from loop. Pin to the Knotting Board.

Step 2

Following the directions for the Square Knot on page 10, make a series of 6 Square Knots. Leaving a small space in-between, make another series of 6 Square Knots.

Step 3

Bring the 2 center threads up and put them through the space in-between the 2 series of 6 Square Knots. Pull tight to form a raised picot, or small loop.

Step 4

Bring threads back to position and, leaving a small space in-between, make 6 more Square Knots. Repeat Step 3. Continue until bracelet is half finished.

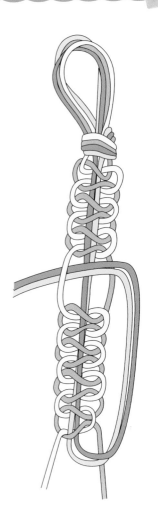

Step 5

Take metal word plate and slip onto threads. Continue steps 2 to 4.

Step 6

Tie a knot at the end.

Step 7

Wrap finished bracelet around wrist, slip the loose ends through the loop, and tie a knot.

Square Knot Charm Bracelet

Materials:

Charms, 4 to 6

Embroidery floss, 2 colors

Step 1

Measure and cut 1 strand of each color floss 6 times the desired length of finished bracelet. Fold threads in half, knot approximately 1" below loop. Pin to the Knotting Board.

Step 2

Make a Square Knot using the 2 outside threads. Do not pull the knot tight.

Step 3

Leaving a small space, make a second Square Knot. Do not pull the knot tight.

Step 4

Leaving a small space, make 3 Square Knots. Do not pull the knots tight.

Step 5

Repeat Step 2.

Step 6

Repeat Step 3, stringing a charm onto the left-hand thread, just before it is tied into the second Square Knot.

Step 7

Repeat pattern, adding in charms, until bracelet is of desired length.

Step 8

Tie ends in a knot.

Step 9

Wrap finished bracelet around wrist, slip the loose ends through the loop, and tie a knot.

Heart-to-Heart Square Knot Bracelet

Materials:

Heart bead

Metallic threads, 2 colors

Step 1

Measure and cut 1 strand of each color metallic thread to 6 times the desired length of finished bracelet. Fold in half, knot approximately 1" below loop. Pin to the Knotting Board.

Step 2

Make Square Knots with spaces, as explained in Square Knot instructions on page 10, switching outside knotting threads as shown in diagram.

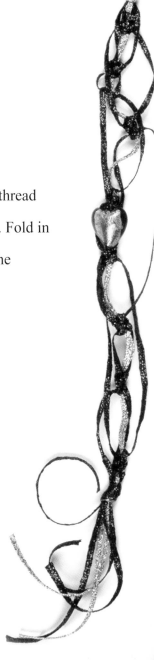

Step 3

Repeat Step 2 until you reach the middle of the bracelet. Thread bead onto two middle threads, then continue with Step 2 pattern until bracelet is of desired length.

Step 4

Knot the end of the bracelet.

Step 5

Wrap finished bracelet around wrist, slip the loose ends through the loop, and tie a knot.

Designer Style: For a variation, use embroidery floss and add beads at random.

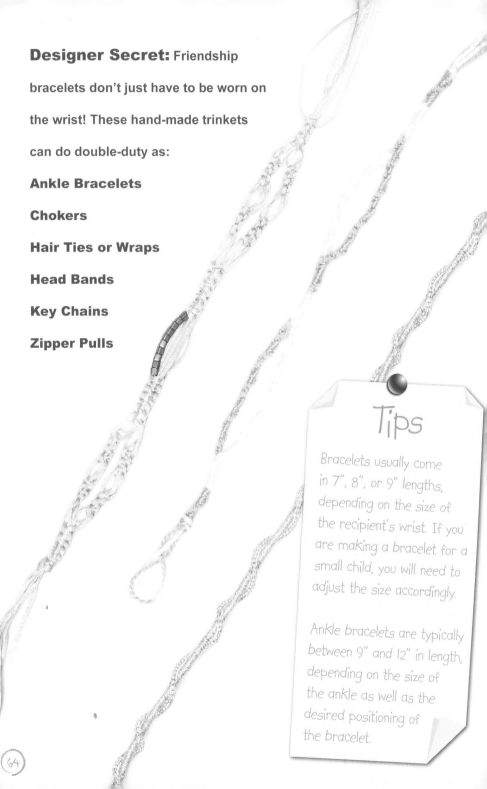

Designer Secret: Friendship bracelets don't just have to be worn on the wrist! These hand-made trinkets can do double-duty as:

Ankle Bracelets

Chokers

Hair Ties or Wraps

Head Bands

Key Chains

Zipper Pulls

Tips

Bracelets usually come in 7", 8", or 9" lengths, depending on the size of the recipient's wrist. If you are making a bracelet for a small child, you will need to adjust the size accordingly.

Ankle bracelets are typically between 9" and 12" in length, depending on the size of the ankle as well as the desired positioning of the bracelet.